# PAPER GOODS
# PROJECTS

# PAPER GOODS PROJECTS

**Coffee Filter Flowers, Doily Butterflies, Cupcake Paper Cards, and 57 More Crafts**

## JODI LEVINE

PHOTOGRAPHS BY **AMY GROPP FORBES**

FOREWORD BY JORDAN FERNEY

POTTER CRAFT

NEW YORK

**FOR ALL THE CRAFTY KIDS OUT THERE,
ESPECIALLY SAMMY, LIONEL, OWEN, OLIVER,
AND BEATRICE!**

Copyright © 2015 by Jodi Levine
Photographs copyright © 2015 by Amy Gropp Forbes

All rights reserved.
Published in the United States by
Potter Craft, an imprint of the
Crown Publishing Group, a division
of Penguin Random House LLC, New York.
www.crownpublishing.com
www.pottercraft.com

POTTER CRAFT and colophon are registered trademarks
of Penguin Random House LLC.

Library of Congress Cataloging-in-Publication data is
available upon request.

ISBN 978-0-8041-8695-7
eBook ISBN 978-0-8041-8696-4

Printed in China

Book design by Robin Rosenthal
Cover photographs by Amy Gropp Forbes

10 9 8 7 6 5 4 3 2 1

First Edition

TABLE OF CONTENTS

# FOREWORD

**THE FIRST RULE OF CRAFTING** is Don't Drop the Glitter. The second rule of crafting is Keep it Simple. It takes more finesse and skill to make a simple project than one that is expensive and time-consuming. After two decades of working on the staff of Martha Stewart, Jodi Levine has mastered the art of clever yet effortless ideas. Jodi is a crafting legend. I remember seeing her genius projects on the pages of magazines when I was planning my own wedding. Her style is fresh yet familiar.

As a craft blogger at the website Oh Happy Day!, I've always thought the best craft projects are the kind that are easy, accessible, and uncontrived. The kind that make you say, "Why didn't I think of that?" *Paper Goods Projects* is so innovative that it had me shaking my head and repeating those words on every page.

*Paper Goods Projects* is the epitome of uncomplicated fun: clever enough to impress any PTA committee, but easy enough to make with kids. Jodi has taken simple techniques and materials, like balloons and cardboard, and reimagined them into new creations that have never been seen before. The supplies for the projects are common and can be found around the house or at any grocery store, but the ideas are brilliant enough to compete with the best Pinterest has to offer.

The projects in this book will add surprise and delight to holidays and celebrations throughout the year. *Paper Goods Projects* is a reminder that the best ideas are simple and right in front of you.

—Jordan Ferney, creator of OhHappyDay.com

# INTRODUCTION

**COLLECTING PAPER GOODS,** like bags, plates, and doilies, and searching the aisles of supermarkets and hardware and variety stores for supplies to use for craft projects have been lifelong passions of mine. Maybe it all started because there weren't craft superstores back when I was a kid (and certainly not websites). I still find so much inspiration in everyday materials and I'm excited to have gathered the fruits of my years of collecting and making things into this book!

As a craft editor at *Martha Stewart Living* magazine for nineteen years, I worked on many everyday material–themed craft stories. My colleagues and I created no-sew Halloween costumes and challenged ourselves to use only nontraditional, nonfabric materials. We created black garbage bag witches, a coffee filter fairy, a paper doily princess, a brown bag cowboy, a flapper in a dress trimmed with cupcake paper scallops, and a knight made with disposable baking tins. As editorial director of *Martha Stewart Kids*, I featured a craft story in each issue, where my staff and I celebrated everyday materials like tin cans, cardboard boxes, and Popsicle sticks. Transforming these materials became my favorite challenge.

Just as every preschool teacher knows, everyday supermarket supplies are not only cheap, plentiful, and easy to find, but transforming them helps us retain the youthful skill to see the potential in things. It's the ability to see the world differently, not to look at a bottle cap as garbage but as a mini frying pan for a doll, or a paper towel tube as a giraffe, waiting to be snipped out. *Paper Goods Projects* is all about that process, because the projects included here are based on materials that you most likely already have in your pantry or recycling bin.

After many years of thinking about doing a crafty food book, I fell in love with the photographs that my longtime friend and former colleague Amy Gropp Forbes was posting on her blog *Eclectic Mom,* and I asked her to partner with me. We had worked together on many kids' stories when she was a food editor at *Martha Stewart Living,* but our friendship deepened when we found out that not only were we pregnant with our firstborns at the same time, but that we even shared the same due date! We both love crafting and cooking with our kids and talked for weeks about the idea of doing a book together. We agreed that crafts using accessible supermarket materials were really at the heart of what we wanted to do and our collaborative project, *Super Make-It*, was born. Our first book, *Candy Aisle Crafts*, came out in August 2014 and contains ideas for edible projects made from common supermarket sweets.

*Paper Goods Projects* is full of project ideas for rainy days, parties, and holidays that adults and kids can do separately or together. We hope you enjoy it!

coffee

FILTERS

+

CUPCAKE

PAPERS

**MANY YEARS AGO,** while working on a costume story in my job as a craft editor at *Martha Stewart Living,* I was shopping for **supplies at the supermarket.** We were doing a story about no-sew costumes, and I was thinking about other materials at the supermarket that could help us with our mission. I spotted some coffee filters, which reminded me of ruffled Elizabethan collars and cuffs. I picked up a few boxes and, after many trips to the store later for more and more coffee filters, we had a couture ruffly ball gown skirt and accessories. Martha loved it and teased me for not wearing it to my wedding. I kind of wish I had!

That was my introduction to the **versatility of coffee filters** as a craft medium. They are meant to get wet, so they take to dyeing very well. Cupcake papers—**coffee filters' little cousins**—are also an excellent crafting material. They come in several sizes: large (often called "Texas muffin" papers), standard, mini, and candy. Recently there has been an explosion in the market of cute patterned and colored cupcake papers. At many online specialty baking supply stores you can find cupcake papers in an **endless array of patterns,** in all colors of the rainbow, scalloped and die-cut edges, and so much more. We have (mostly) used the very widely available pastel- and solid-colored papers found at supermarkets, with a few exceptions. Note that it is worth checking your local party store, where they are likely to have a great selection.

## GENERAL COFFEE FILTER AND CUPCAKE PAPER DYEING TIPS

To prepare the dye, fill a pie pan or shallow baking dish with about an inch of water. Squeeze a few drops of food coloring into the water, and stir well.

**For most of these crafts, the filters and cupcake papers should remain ruffled. To retain ruffliness, dye a stack of at least fifteen to twenty coffee filters or three to four cupcake papers at the same time. Dip the stack of coffee filters into the dye as quickly as possible (the moisture will start to flatten the ruffles). Cupcake papers can sit in dye longer—a few minutes or as long as needed. Place the stack of dyed ruffles onto a baking sheet that has been lined with paper towels, newspaper, or cardboard boxes to absorb excess dye and protect surfaces.**

**Don't worry if the filters are splotchy once they're dry. Often the outer layer is unevenly dyed but the inside filters have been dyed nicely.**

**The coffee filters can take a long time to dry, depending on the thickness of the stack that was dyed. Let them dry overnight.**

# COFFEE FILTER WATER LILY TABLE SETTING

These coffee filter water lilies involve a few steps, but none of them is tricky. Once you get the hang of it you'll be able to make lots of them fast! They're beautiful on top of dyed-green flat coffee filter lily pads running down the center of a table—perfect for a Mother's Day brunch or a shower.

**SUPPLIES**
**food coloring**

**coffee filters**

**scissors**

**white glue**

**paintbrush and small bowl**

**pencil (optional)**

**small plate or roll of tape (optional)**

**1.** Dip-dye a stack of coffee filters in floral colors, dyeing the centers only (as shown), edges only, or solid, and retaining the ruffles (see at left for dyeing instructions). Let them dry completely, about three hours to overnight.

**2.** When they're dry, separate the filters into stacks of three. For one flower you will need three filters dyed in one color and one filter dyed in a contrasting color for the flower stamen. Fold a stack in half and then in half twice more (into eighths). Trim the top into a petal shape (A).

**3.** Unfold and pull one filter off the stack. Take the remaining stack of two, refold, and trim ¼" off the petal shape. Pull off another filter. Take the remaining filter, refold, and trim another ¼" off the petal shape (B).

**4.** In all three filters, cut a slit along one fold to the center point. Take the medium-sized filter and cut out one petal. Cut two petals out of the smallest filter (C).

**5.** Take one filter and lightly brush white glue on one of the petals at the slit (D). Pull the other petal across the slit to overlap onto the glued petal. This will create a cupped shape. Repeat with the remaining two filters. Press your finger into the center of each cupped filter to make a flat bottom.

**6.** Lightly brush white glue on the inside center of the largest filter and press the medium-sized filter onto the glue.

Glue the small filter inside the medium-sized filter. Rotate the layers so the petals are staggered (E). Also, as you glue the top two layers together, place the heavy seam sides opposite each other so the flower won't tilt over.

**7.** To make the stamen, take the dyed filter in a contrasting color and cut off a 1½" ruffled strip (F). Accordion-fold the strip in 2" folds. Cut halfway into the top of the strip to make fringe, and then trim the fringes into pointy hairiness. Unfold and twist, rolling tightly at the bottom, as shown, and brushing glue along the bottom as you go. Twist to secure. Snip off the bottom until the stamen is about ¾" tall. Glue the bottom into the center of the flower.

**8.** If you want to make the lily pads, dye coffee filters in different shades of green. Let them dry flat. Trim to different-sized circles. (Trace circles using a small plate or a roll of tape as a circle template.)

**9.** Arrange the lily pads on a table, and place the flowers on top of them.

A

D

# COOKIE FAVOR FLOWERS

Dress up a plain cookie as a pretty party favor with an easy-to-make flower. Meringue cookies, either homemade or the premade ones that are widely available in tubs at supermarkets, work well because they aren't greasy and come in light colors. Another option is a small sack of candy.

**SUPPLIES**

**pink, yellow, and green food coloring**

**coffee filters**

**scissors**

**smooth string (such as baker's twine)**

**nontoxic white glue or adhesive dots**

**1.** Dip-dye the edges of a stack of coffee filters pink or yellow (see page 14 for instructions) and dye another stack solid green. Let dry completely, about three hours to overnight.

**2.** To make the leaves, take a stack of about three green coffee filters. Cut into the stack edge in an arc shape, as shown.

Fold the stack in half, and separate into individual leaves.

**3.** Put a cookie in the center of a single pink or yellow coffee filter. Gather the top and twist. Tie a string (do not knot) under the flower, and pull the ends to cinch. Undo and remove the string. The flower should stay in place.

**4.** Attach the leaf to a flower with a dot of white glue or an adhesive dot underneath the flower petal.

# COFFEE FILTER FLOWERS

There are many ways to transform coffee filters into flowers, but this might be the very easiest. It is the perfect technique when you want a craft for small children or you need flowers in multiples for something like garlands or party favor bags.

**SUPPLIES**
**unbleached or dyed (see page 14) coffee filters**

**1.** Make a circle with your index finger and thumb. With your other hand, take a coffee filter and poke another finger into the center of the filter, pushing it down through the circle of your fingers.

**2.** Grab the bottom of the filter and pull it down through the circle. Twist the now-pointed bottom of the filter, leaving the top open and flowery.

## FLOWER FAVOR BAG AND GARLAND

*These natural-colored flowers look great paired with a brightly colored string, like the neon string called Mason's twine, available at hardware stores.*

**SUPPLIES**
**brown lunch bags (for favor bags only)**

**hole punch (for favor bags only)**

**string (such as neon Mason's twine)**

**Coffee Filter Flowers (see above)**

**1.** To make a favor bag, fill a brown lunch bag with party favor items. Fold the top flap down about 3". Punch two holes in the folded top and thread a piece of string through the holes. Tie on a flower. Knot the ends of the string and let them unravel into fringe.

**2.** To make the garland, tie the flowers along your desired length of string. (Make sure you allow a few feet of extra string for knotting.)

## COFFEE FILTER FLOWER NAPKIN RINGS

*I love any way to reuse toilet paper and paper towel tubes. A pile of rolled-up napkins with these rings would look pretty on a buffet table.*

**SUPPLIES**
scissors

**paper towel or toilet paper tube**

**hole punch**

**Coffee Filter Flowers (page 20)**

**hot glue (or white glue)**

**coffee filter leaves (see page 18)**

**1.** Cut the cardboard tubes into 1½" rings. Punch a hole in the center of one of the rings, and pull the twisted bottom of a flower through the hole. Trim off a bit of the twisty tail, keeping a ½" or so stub. Hot-glue the twisty stub to the inside of the ring. Repeat with the remaining rings and flowers.

**2.** Hot-glue a leaf or two under each flower.

## COFFEE FILTER FLOWER STRAWS

*Use green-striped-paper or solid-green-plastic straws. These garnishes will make iced tea a bit more festive!*

**SUPPLIES**
scissors

**Coffee Filter Flowers (page 20)**

**hot glue**

**solid-green-plastic or green-striped-paper (or any!) straws**

**coffee filter leaves (see page 18)**

**1.** Snip off some of the flower's twisty bottom, leaving ½" or so as a stub. Squeeze some nontoxic hot glue onto the flower and the stub, and press the flower against the straw, leaving at least an inch at the top of the straw for sipping.

**2.** Squeeze a little bit of glue onto the pointy side of a leaf, and wrap the leaf around the flower bottom to cover it.

# BIRD, CLOUDS, AND TREES CAKE

Little cupcake paper trees, birds, and clouds make a sweet scene
for a holiday, a wintertime baby shower, or a birthday cake. I love that
the topper is taller than the cake itself.

**SUPPLIES**

**3 white cupcake papers
(I used Texas-style large muffin
papers, but standard-size
work, too)**

**scissors**

**white glue, hot glue, or
adhesive dots**

**12"-long wooden skewers**

**3 to 9 green cupcake papers**

**1.** To make the clouds, fold one
white cupcake paper in half.
Cut out the round middle, and
cut the ridged edges into strips.
Cut cloud shapes out of the
strips and glue the clouds to
the tops of the skewers.

**2.** To make the bird, fold two
cupcake papers in half. Use the
template on page 100 to cut
a bird body shape (the top
of the bird is along the fold)
and two wing shapes. Glue
the skewer to the inside of
the bird body, as shown, and
glue a wing on either side.

**3.** To make the tree, cut one
green cupcake paper in
half. Lightly fold to make a
center mark on the straight cut
side. Place adhesive dots or
lightly brush glue along one
half of the top straight side.
Form a cone shape by
overlapping the unglued
straight edge over the glued
edge. Repeat with the
remaining two cupcake
papers. (For a multitiered tree,
stack a few cones on top of
each other.)

# CUPCAKE PAPER FLOWER PETIT FOUR TOPPERS

Cupcake paper flowers and a poured confectioner's sugar glaze dress up small-cut cubes of sheet cake into pretty petits fours.

### SUPPLIES

**standard or mini cupcake papers in floral colors**

**hot glue or white glue**

**standard or mini cupcake papers in leaf colors**

**scissors**

**petits fours**

**frosting (optional)**

**1.** To make the flowers, fold the floral-colored papers in half and in half again.

**2.** Stick a finger inside one of the layers to push it open. Fold a triangular flap underneath to give the flower a flat bottom. Use the hot glue—or have kids use white glue—to secure the flap down.

**3.** To make the leaves, fold a green cupcake paper in half and in half again. Open it and cut along the folds so that you have four pieces. Cut each piece into a leaf shape, as shown. Glue a leaf under the flower with hot or white glue.

**4.** Place flowers on top of the little cakes before the icing has hardened or top store-bought cakes by adding a dot of frosting with a toothpick to adhere the flower.

## CUPCAKE PAPER NECKLACE

### SUPPLIES

**standard or mini cupcake papers in floral colors**

**scissors**

**hot or white glue**

**standard or mini cupcake papers in leaf colors**

**string (such as striped baker's twine; optional)**

**blunt sewing needle with a large eye (often called tapestry or darning needle)**

**1.** Fold a floral-colored cupcake paper in half and in half again.

**2.** Cut the ridged edge into thirds. Cut into the ridged folded edges as well.

**3.** Round out the bottoms of these flaps into a petal shape.

**4.** Open the fold so that it is folded in half. Twist the bottom, and put a finger inside the flower to spread the petals. Fold a tiny triangle at the base to secure the twist, and hot-glue it closed.

**5.** Make leaves following the instructions in step 3 at left.

**6.** Cut a piece of string long enough so that once knotted it will easily slip over the child's head. Thread the needle with the string. Use the needle to poke through the twisted bottom of the flowers. Knot the two ends together.

**7.** Hot-glue a leaf or two under each flower.

# BLUE AND GREEN CUPCAKE PAPER CARDS AND TAGS

These little cards and tags take advantage of cupcake papers' ruffled texture. I always seem to have a few stray cupcake papers left over from various packs, and this is a nice use for them.

A

B

C

## SUPPLIES
scissors

assorted cupcake papers, in various colors and sizes

aluminum foil (optional)

white glue

blank tags and cards

rubber stamps and ink, sticker letters, or pens

baker's twine

assorted paper circles (punched or store-bought confetti) or sticker dots

hole punch (optional)

sticker star (optional)

**1. CLOUDS** Cut out cloud shapes from large white cupcake papers. Cut raindrops out of a silver cupcake paper (or aluminum foil). Glue the clouds and raindrops to a tag or card, and stamp on a message.

**2. HEART TAG** Cut a heart shape out of a cupcake paper. Glue it onto a tag, and stamp an initial inside.

**3. BUNTING** (A) Glue a bit of baker's twine to a tag or card. Cut out a few triangles from a cupcake paper and glue them onto the twine. Stamp on a name or message.

**4. ICE CREAM CONE** Cut out a little triangle from a cupcake paper for the cone. Add confetti circles (or punch or hand-cut dots) for the scoops. Glue the dots to the card, and then glue on the cone.

**5. WHITE AND GREEN CHRISTMAS TREES** (B) Cut two triangles out of a cupcake paper. Cut a trapezoid shape out of a silver cupcake paper (or aluminum foil) for the planter. Glue the bottom tree

layer onto the card and then glue on the top layer and the planter. Top with a sticker star, if desired.

**6. BIRD** Fold a cupcake paper in half. Trace the template on page 100 (the top of the bird will be along the folded edge). Cut out the bird and wing shapes and glue onto a card.

**7. FATHER'S DAY TIE** (C) Cut a tie and collar shape (see the templates on page 106). Glue the top of the tie to the top of the card and glue the top of the white collar pieces over it, as shown (rather than gluing it down flat, so it retains dimension). Stamp or write a message.

1 SHOWER

2 F

3 SAM

7 HAPPY FATHERS DAY

4

5

6

5

# CUPCAKE PAPER DOLLHOUSE ACCESSORIES

These little dollhouse accessories are fast and easy to make; a perfect playdate activity. For greater strength or opacity, double or triple the cupcake papers.

**SUPPLIES**
standard or mini cupcake papers in various colors

adhesive dots or double-sided tape

white glue

scissors

toothpick and blue paper (optional, for curtains)

wooden peg people (available at craft stores) or small dolls or animal figures

round wooden clothespin (for lamp)

inner box of a small matchbox (for crib)

small colored paper napkin (for crib mattress and blanket)

**1. Lampshade** Attach a mini cupcake paper to the top of the clothespin with an adhesive dot or small piece of double-sided tape.

**2. Chair** The base is a stack of 2 upside-down mini cupcake papers. To make the chair back, cut out a semi-circle piece from the ruffled edge of a mini cupcake paper, leaving it attached to the flat round cupcake bottom. Brush white glue on the top of the chair base and adhere the flat bottom of the chair back piece to it.

**3. Crib** Cut out the center of 2 regular cupcake papers so you are left with 2 ruffled strips. Press a few adhesive dots or some double-sided tape around the outside edge of the matchbox and wrap and adhere the bottom of the ribbed cupcake paper to it. Patch on an additional piece of cupcake paper as needed to cover and encircle the box. Cut out a little rectangle from the paper napkin for the crib mattress and a smaller piece for a crib blanket.

**4. Mom's Skirt** Cut out the center of a regular cupcake paper so you are left with a ruffled strip. Wrap it around the mom's waist and adhere it with an adhesive dot at back.

**5. Dad's Collar** Cut a circle out of the center of a mini cupcake paper and fit it around the dad's neck. Trim off the ribbed edge leaving 2 triangles that look like a "bib" front.

**6. Curtains** Cut a 2 x 2 1/2" piece of blue paper. Cut out the center of a regular cupcake paper so you are left with a ruffled strip. Cut the strip in half vertically and then trim it horizontally into thirds to get six 1 1/4"-tall pieces. Glue 3 pieces together, as shown, and repeat with remaining 3 pieces to make a second curtain panel. Glue the tops of the curtains to the toothpick. Glue the toothpick to the short end of the blue paper and adhere the whole thing to the dollhouse wall with double-sided tape.

PAPER
PLATES
BAGS
+
DOILIES

**WHEN I WAS A KID,** my friend's mother took care of me occasionally while my mom worked. I'm not sure how it started, but according to my friend and her mom, all I wanted to do was make paper plate clocks. Every day. The kind we made at school with brass paper fasteners. I still love the **classic fluted-edge paper plates** and see lots of crafty potential in them. We include just a few of the many possibilities in this chapter, along with projects that use a couple of our other favorite paper supermarket products: paper bags and doilies.

Oh, how I loved **doilies** as a kid! At all her holiday meals, my aunt Elaine reliably served fruit cocktail in a footed glass atop a paper doily. I hope she never noticed that I went around the table and collected them for my own use. Not something that we ever had in my house, doilies were precious and—I thought—**very, very fancy.**

As a kid I figured that the plain brown bags I wanted for puppetmaking or other crafts were something that you had to luck upon. When I got a little older, I couldn't believe my good fortune when I found that supermarkets sell packs of them. Now I love them for **inexpensive and blank-slate** favor bags for my kids' parties, and I'm happy to even see them available in white and a few colors at big box stores (and lots of colors and sizes at craft stores and online).

# FLORAL PAPER PLATE PLATTERS

These simple paper plate flowers can also be used to decorate the dessert stands on page 36. Like the stands, these platters are perfect for a child's birthday or tea party or a shower.

**SUPPLIES**
scissors

**large and small paper plates**

**pencil**

**hot glue, white glue, or adhesive dots**

**1.** To make the flowers, cut out the flat center of a large paper plate. (Save the ribbed edge for making leaves.) Draw some flowers or see the template on page 100. Cut out the flowers.

**2.** To make the leaves, cut out sections of four to seven ribs (depending on the size of the leaf) from the fluted edge of a paper plate, one for each leaf. Fold in half, against the ribs. Cut the piece into a leaf shape.

**3.** Glue the flowers and leaves to the plates.

# PAPER PLATE DESSERT STANDS

These little dessert stands are perfect for a play tea party. Made from paper plates, paper cups, and nut cups, they come together quickly and are ready to decorate with the paper flowers shown here (which are also made from paper plates) or anything your kids desire. They are best for lightweight items like meringues, mini cupcakes, petits fours, tea sandwiches, and little candies.

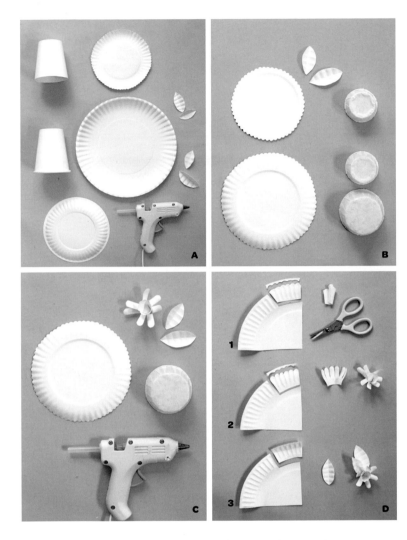

scalloped scissors, and glue one of them, upside down, on top. Glue another small nut cup, upside down, on top of the plate, and then top with the remaining trimmed small plate, glued upside down.

**3.** To make the small stand (C), invert a large nut cup. Trim a small paper plate with scalloped scissors and glue it, upside down, to the nut cup.

# PAPER PLATE FLOWERS

**SUPPLIES**
scissors

**1 paper plate**
**scalloped scissors**
**hot glue**

**1.** To make the flowers, cut out a section of six ribs from the fluted edge of a paper plate (D1). Trim around the top of the ribs to make a scalloped edge. Roll the fluted six-rib section of the plate into a loose cone for the flower's trumpet center and glue to secure.

**2.** Cut a six-rib section from the plate, with about ½" extra at the bottom (D2). Trim around the edge to create a scallop, and then cut in between each rib (not all the way) to make petals. Glue one bottom end of the petals to the trumpet center, wrap it around, and glue again.

**3.** To make the leaves (D3), cut out sections of six ribs (or fewer or more, depending on the size of the leaf) off the fluted edge of a paper plate, one for each leaf. Fold in half, against the ribs. Cut the piece into a leaf shape. Glue one or two leaves to the bottom of the flower.

**SUPPLIES**
**paper cups**

**hot glue, white glue, or adhesive dots**

**paper plates, small and large**

**Paper Plate Flowers (at right)**

**nut cups, small and large (optional)**

**scalloped scissors (optional)**

**scissors**

**1.** To make the large stand (A), turn over two paper cups. Glue one cup on top of an overturned small paper plate for the base. (Right before gluing, make sure that everything is centered. Check from a few angles.) On top of the cup glue a large paper plate. Glue the other paper cup on the large paper plate, and then glue a small paper plate on the very top. Embellish the stand with Paper Plate Flowers.

**2.** To make the medium-sized stand (B), turn one large nut cup upside down, and glue one small nut cup, upside down, on top of it. (If you can't find nut cups, cut down a paper cup.) Trim two small plates with

# PAPER PLATE MASKS

These masks utilize the ribbed edges of inexpensive paper plates to create a furry lion's mane, ruffled feathers, and bushy mustaches and beards. The plates are sold coated (slightly shiny) and uncoated (matte). I recommend using coated for their sturdiness, if you can find them, but either will work.

## LION

**SUPPLIES**
**craft knife**

**scissors**

**two 9" paper plates**

**orange and black craft paint**

**paintbrushes**

**hot glue**

**½" dowel, cut to about 15" long**

**1.** Using the craft knife or scissors, poke a starter hole in the center of the paper plate. Cut out the flat center circle.

**2.** Using the templates on page 103, trace and cut ears along the ruffled edge of the second plate. Cut six 4½"-long skinny strips out of the center of this plate for whiskers.

**3.** Paint the mask plate and ears orange and the whiskers black; let dry.

**4.** Glue the ears and whiskers onto the mask plate.

**5.** Glue the dowel onto the back of one side of the mask.

## BIRD

**SUPPLIES**
**four 9" paper plates**

**scissors**

**pencil**

**craft knife**

**hot glue**

**yellow craft paint**

**paintbrushes**

**½" dowel, cut to about 15" long**

**1.** Cut the mask base: Trim 3" off the bottom of one plate so you are left with a piece of plate that's slightly larger than half. The cut bottom will be the bottom of the mask. Fold the sides in about ¾" and glue them behind the mask. Measure the eye width of the wearer, pencil eyes on the mask, and cut out the eye holes with a craft knife.

**2.** Cut out 16 feathers (use the leaf templates on page 100) along the ribbed edge of two of the plates, ranging in size from 2½" to 3" long and about ¾" to 1¼" wide. Fold them in half perpendicular to the ribbing (press them against a table edge to help get a sharp crease).

**3.** Cut two skinny semicircle pieces along the ribbed edge of a plate for the beak, about 7" long and 2¼" at its widest. Fold down ½" of the plate along the long cut edge on both pieces. Apply glue to these flaps and adhere them together to create the beak. Snip off about 1" from one pointy end of the beak. Glue that cut end to the bottom of the mask base.

**4.** Paint the feathers and the mask base and beak; let dry.

**5.** Glue the feathers to the mask base.

**6.** Glue the dowel onto the back of one side of the mask.

## BUNNY

**SUPPLIES**

two 9" paper plates

scissors

pencil

craft knife

pink and black craft paint

paintbrushes

hot glue

½" dowel, cut to 15" long

**1.** Cut a slit in one of the plates along the radius to the center. Measure the width of the wearer's eyes. Overlap the slits about 2" and hold in place while you pencil in the eye holes to your desired width, positioning them so that they are centered above the seam that will be at the bottom. Let go of the overlapping seam so the plate is flat again and cut out the eyes with the craft knife. Overlap the slits again and glue closed.

**2.** Cut out two ears from the ribbed edge of the second plate, about 6" long and 1¾" at the widest point. Fold each ear in half (press them against a table edge to help get a sharp crease).

**3.** Cut out an oval, about ¾" x ½" from a scrap of the ribbed edge for a nose. Cut six skinny strips, about 3" long, for whiskers.

**4.** Paint the ears and the face mask pink and the nose and whiskers black; let dry.

**5.** Glue the ears behind the top of the mask, the whiskers to the center point, and the nose on top of them.

**6.** Glue the dowel onto the back of one side of the mask.

## FACES

(see photograph on page 2)

**SUPPLIES**

two to three 9" paper plates

one 6" paper plate (optional, for beard)

craft knife

scissors

pink or blue and black craft paint

paintbrushes

hot glue

½" dowel, cut to 15" long

**1.** Measure the width of the wearer's eyes. Pencil eyes onto a 9" plate and cut them out with the craft knife.

**2.** Make a nose: Cut out a wedge, between 4½" and 6" long and 3½" and 5" wide from the other plate for a nose. Fold the wedge in half. Fold ¼" flaps along either side. Glue the flaps of the nose onto the mask.

**3.** Make eyebrows and eyelashes (optional): Cut two skinny "leaf"-shaped eyebrows along the ribbed edge of second plate. Cut two trapezoidal eyelash pieces off the ribbed edge, about 2¼" wide and 1¼" tall. Fold down a ¼" flap for gluing onto the mask.

**4.** Make a mustache: Cut a trapezoidal or skinny semicircle along the ribbed edge of the second plate scrap, about 4½" to 5½" wide and 1¼" to 2¼" tall.

**5.** Make a beard (optional): Cut ½" or so off the top of a 6" paper plate.

**6.** Make ears (optional): Cut two semicircles off the ribbed edge of the second or third 9" plate, about 1½" deep and 2½" tall.

**7.** Paint the face and ears (optional) and the eyebrows, mustache, eyelashes, and beard (optional); let dry.

**8.** Glue the pieces into place on the mask.

**9.** Glue the dowel onto the back of one side of the mask.

# DOILY TIARA AND PETER PAN COLLAR

These easy-to-make accessories are fun for last-minute Halloween costumes, a fancy tea party, or everyday dress-up play.

## PETER PAN COLLAR

**SUPPLIES**
scissors

**1 small (6") paper plate**

scissors

**two 4" doilies**

**white glue**

**Velcro dots**

**1.** Cut a collar base using the same technique as for making the headband for the Doily Tiara but with only one layer (see step 2, at left). Turn the plate collar base upside down (B).

**2.** Cut the two doilies in half. Glue the two halves as a collar onto the paper plate base. Cut the other two doily halves down slightly to shorten them. Glue the two shorter doilies on top of the first ones.

**3.** Add a Velcro dot to close the collar back (cut the dot smaller, if necessary).

## DOILY TIARA

**SUPPLIES**
white glue

**2 small (6") paper plates**

scissors

**scalloped scissors (optional)**

**one 10" doily**

**1.** Glue the two small plates together, nesting them so they fit one on top of the other. This will make a sturdier headband base (A). Let dry.

**2.** Cut the solid center out of the glued-together paper plates. Use scalloped or regular scissors to cut a headband that's about ⅝" at its widest, as shown.

**3.** Cut the solid center out of the doily, leaving the thin strip of paper that holds the lace together, as shown. Cut away the doily lace to create a tiara shape. Glue on extra cut pieces of lace at top, if desired, to customize the tiara.

**4.** Squeeze a thin line of glue onto the flat rimmed edge of the paper plate headband and put the doily lace on top. Let dry.

# DOILY BUTTERFLIES

Doily butterflies are perfect decorations for favor bags at a bridal or baby shower, or a princess party. Try using a variety of doily types for this project. "Medallion" lace doilies have an all-over lace pattern and no white solid center. Look carefully at the doily to find parts of the design that, once cut out, will work as wings.

**SUPPLIES**
**doilies**

**scissors**

**white glue**

**adhesive dots**

**string (optional)**

**1.** Find a section of a doily that has two attached motifs—or two that could be glued together—that could work as the top and bottom of each wing. Cut out a wing (or the pieces for one wing), find that same motif (or motifs) in a mirror image on the other side of the doily, and cut a second wing out. Glue the wing pieces together, if needed, and repeat for a second wing.

**2.** Glue the two wings together; let dry.

**3.** Fold the butterfly at the center. Attach to a favor bag with an adhesive dot.

**4.** Make a garland (optional): Thread some string through the butterflies and a few doily flowers (page 46) to make a garland.

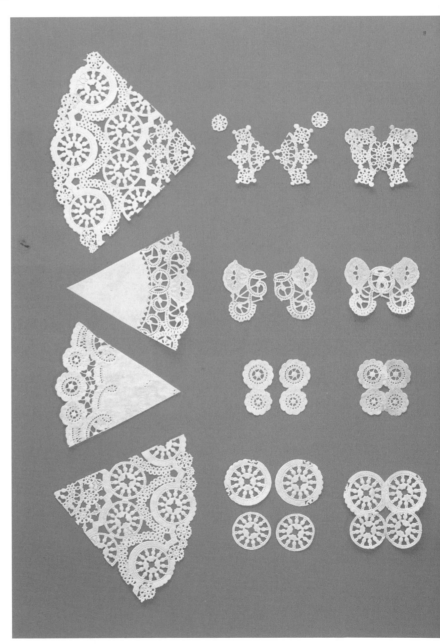

# DOILY FLOWER GIFT TOPPERS

Mixing and matching two easy techniques with different sizes and styles of doilies will allow you to create an endless variety of flowers. Try making them with both all-over lace doilies (aka "medallion" lace) and doilies with solid paper centers. There are many uses for these: Glue to a toothpick or skewer for a cute cake or cupcake topper, string on thin twine to make a flower garland, or attach to a favor bag.

**SUPPLIES**
doilies

scissors

paintbrush

white glue

adhesive dots

string (optional)

**1. BOWL STYLE:** Cut out a 2" pie piece (or larger for more of a cupped /trumpet shape) from a doily and discard the wedge. Brush glue on one side of the cut and overlap the pieces to form a bowl, matching the motifs on either side to hide the seam.

**2. PETAL STYLE:** Like making a snowflake (or a water lily, page 14), fold a doily in half and then in thirds so the doily is divided into six pie pieces or in half and then half again so that your circle is divided into eight pie pieces. While it is still folded, using scissors, trim the open end into a rounded petal shape. Open up the doily. Cut a slit into the center and overlap and glue two petals to give the doily a cupped shape.

**3.** Create different sizes of the bowl flower. Layer a small bowl flower into the center of a larger petal or bowl style flower. Attach with an adhesive dot or white glue. Adhere three small bowl flowers together with adhesive dots, as on the light pink present, top right.

**4.** Make a garland (optional): Thread doily scraps on a string to make a garland (as on dark pink gift, middle left).

# HOUSE FAVOR BAGS

Have your child help decorate these favor bags with window and door cardboard cutouts. Party guests can play with these and won't even know until the end of the festivities that there are favors inside! Or simply make these as toys and fill them with scrunched-up newspaper.

## SUPPLIES
brown bags

paint

paintbrushes

scissors

cardboard packaging scraps

white glue, double-sided tape, or adhesive dots

party favors

Velcro dots (optional)

**1.** With the smooth side of a bag facing up (seam side on the back) fold the top corners to the back to make a pointy roof.

**2.** Paint the roofs or house fronts. (You can do this with the bag standing up, as shown, or you can lay them flat.) Let them dry.

**3.** Cut doors and windows out of the cardboard packaging scraps.

**4.** Glue or tape on the doors and windows.

**5.** Open the folded roof flap and fill with the party favor(s). Refold and close with an adhesive dot or a Velcro dot, if you want the bags to be resealable.

# BROWN BAG PAPER PARTY HATS

Heavyweight kraft paper shopping bags make sturdy party hats.

**SUPPLIES**

scissors

**recycled paper shopping bags**

**paint**

**paintbrushes**

**pencil**

**hot glue, double-sided tape, or adhesive dots**

**1.** Cut open some large brown paper grocery bags. Have your child do some painting on them and let them dry.

**2.** See the template on page 106 or cut open a party hat and trace the shape onto the bag, fitting as many as you can on one bag. Cut out the hats and curl them around to form a hat shape. Glue down one side to close.

# PAPER BAG ANIMAL FAVOR BAGS

Grouped together on clotheslines, these favor bags make a great decoration during a party until it's time for the guests to take them home!

**SUPPLIES**
**brown paper lunch bags**

**pencil**

**scissors**

**scrap cardboard and bags**

**paint**

**paintbrushes**

**dot stickers or punched circles**

**adhesive dots or
double-sided tape**

**party favors**

**Velcro dots (optional)**

**1.** Fold down a flap that is about 3½" to 4" (longer for the bunny). Fold the two bottom corners in to make the flap pointy, as shown (or fold in only one corner, as for the mouse).

**2.** See the templates on pages 106–107 to trace and cut ears, tails, and/or antlers onto scrap cardboard and bags.

**3.** Paint the bags using the photos as a guide. (You can do this with the bag standing up, as shown, or you can lay it flat.) Let them dry completely.

**4.** Use the adhesive dots to glue on the ears, tails, and/or antlers. Add dot stickers and/or punched circle eyes and noses.

**5.** Open the folded flap and fill with party favor(s). Refold and close with an adhesive dot or a Velcro dot, if you want the bags to be resealable.

**BALLOONS MAKE PEOPLE HAPPY** Several years ago I bought a stash of twisty balloons and balloon pumps for my sons' birthday parties. After realizing that **balloon-twisting** loosened up a crowd and created an instant party, I started bringing my stash to family gatherings and reunions too. Though I never learned proper technique, it doesn't seem to matter. We have a pile of balloon pumps, and everyone tries to make **fancy and giant hats and sculptures.** And you don't need a party to do this. I pull out the pumps and twisty balloons often, especially when some shy kids are visiting and I need to help warm everyone up. You won't regret buying an inexpensive balloon pump, often sold alongside twisty balloons with the party supplies in many supermarkets, where you can also find regular round and water balloons.

My laziness about not learning proper balloon-twisting, coupled with my desire to make balloon sculptures, inspired a lot of the projects in this chapter. I was playing with blowing up a round balloon through a toilet paper tube (which cinched it in the center), and it instantly looked like a roly-poly clown. **I realized that all the different shapes and sizes could be stuck together to make all sorts of creatures and more.** Tiny water balloons make perfect clown noses and ballerina buns. If you blow them up only slightly, they become tiny ears on a giraffe, for example (see page 63). The projects that follow are the happy results of my play.

When using twisty balloons, inflate the balloon entirely to get the thickness you want. Pinch where you want the length to end, and release air from that point only. Knot the balloon at the pinched spot.

**Steady a round balloon figure in a circular base made from a twisty balloon.**

**To make eyes, use ¼" round color-coding labels (colored black with a marker), hole-punched black paper or adhesive labels (colored black with a marker), or simply draw them on with a Sharpie. Round color-coding labels and other labels are sold at office supply stores.**

*Balloons are a choking hazard!* **Children under eight years old can choke or suffocate on uninflated or broken balloons. Adult supervision is required. Keep uninflated and broken balloons away from children. Discard broken balloons immediately.**

# CLOWN CAKE TOPPER

A simpler version of the clowns on page 58, these guys make an easy cake topper for a circus-themed party. Alternatively, for a table decoration, they can be displayed in jars filled with sugar or small candies (like jelly beans) to anchor them.

**SUPPLIES**
**balloon pump**
**1 medium or small white balloon**
**straw**
**black dot stickers or permanent marker**
**2 red water balloons**
**scissors**
**adhesive dots**
**1 coffee filter, dyed blue (see page 14)**

**1.** Inflate the white balloon until it is about 5" in diameter, and tie it to a straw. Let it flop down (the knot will be at the back of the head). Stick on the dot stickers as eyes (see General Balloon Crafting Tips, at left, for eye techniques).

**2.** To make the nose, inflate a small red water balloon, and trim the knot. Stick it to the face with an adhesive dot by putting the dot half on and half off the knot so it is not visible.

**3.** To make the hat, cut the dyed coffee filter in half. Inflate the second red water balloon slightly so that you have a small ball, and knot it. Stick the ball to the center of the straight-cut side of the coffee filter with an adhesive dot. Form a cone by overlapping the two halves of the straight edges around the knot, and stick the seams together with an adhesive dot. Attach to the top of the head with another adhesive dot or two.

# BLUE CLOWNS

Decorate a table with a few of these jolly clowns at a circus-themed party.

**SUPPLIES**
**balloon pump**

**2 medium round teal balloons**

**2 red water balloons**

**scissors**

**adhesive dots**

**black dot stickers or permanent marker (see General Balloon Crafting Tips, page 56)**

**1 red twisty balloon**

**2 coffee filters, dyed blue or teal**

**1 teal twisty balloon**

**1.** To make the head and body, inflate one medium teal balloon slightly for the head. Inflate the other medium teal balloon entirely for the body. Slightly inflate one of the red water balloons for the nose; trim the knot, and stick it to the head balloon with an adhesive dot or two. Stick on the dot stickers as eyes or draw on with a permanent marker (see page 56 for eye techniques). To make the mouth, barely inflate the red twisty balloon, knot it to the desired mouth size, and trim the knot. Stick it to the face with two adhesive dots.

**2.** To make the collar, cut out the center of a dyed coffee filter.

**3.** To make the hat, cut a dyed coffee filter in half. Inflate the second red water balloon slightly so that you have a small ball, and knot it. Stick the ball to the center of the straight-cut side of the coffee filter with an adhesive dot. Form a cone by overlapping the two halves of the straight edges around the knot of the balloon, and stick the seams together with an adhesive dot. Attach to the top of the head with another adhesive dot or two.

**4.** Adhere the collar to the top of the medium body balloon with adhesive dots. Adhere the head to the body balloon through the hole in the collar on top of the body.

**5.** To make the base, inflate a teal twisty balloon and curve it into an O-shape. Hold it in place before knotting to see if the round bottom of the clown's body will rest inside the O. Adjust the size, if necessary, tie off, and adhere the ends together with an adhesive dot. Affix the bottom of the clown to the base with adhesive dots.

# STRONGMAN

Hang this rotund balloon strongman over a table at a circus-themed birthday party. As a variation you can make an acrobat by hanging its arms on a straw trapeze (and leaving off the balloon weights).

**SUPPLIES**
**balloon pump**

**1 medium yellow balloon**

**3 yellow twisty balloons**

**adhesive dots**

**scissors**

**1 small yellow balloon (or another medium yellow balloon, barely inflated)**

**black dot stickers or permanent marker**

**¼" × 12" strip of black construction paper**

**pencil**

**2 small black (or purple or dark green) balloons**

**1 straw**

**1.** To make the body, fully inflate the medium yellow balloon and knot it.

**2.** To make the arms, inflate two of the yellow twisty balloons until they are each about 12" long. Knot and trim off the extra length. To make the legs, fully inflate the remaining yellow twisty balloon. Knot it, twist it at the center, and stick the two ends together with an adhesive dot.

**3.** To make the head, slightly inflate the small (or medium) yellow balloon, knot it, and trim the knot. Stick on the black dot stickers for eyes. Curl the ends of the black construction paper strip by winding it around a pencil and then unwinding. Stick it to the face with an adhesive dot.

**4.** Attach the legs, arms, and head to the body balloon with adhesive dots.

**5.** To make the dumbbells, inflate the two small black balloons, knot them, and trim the knot. Wrap an adhesive dot around both ends of a straw. Feed the sticky end of the straw into the balloon knot. Repeat on the other side.

**6.** Stick the dumbbell to the "hands" of the strongman with adhesive dots.

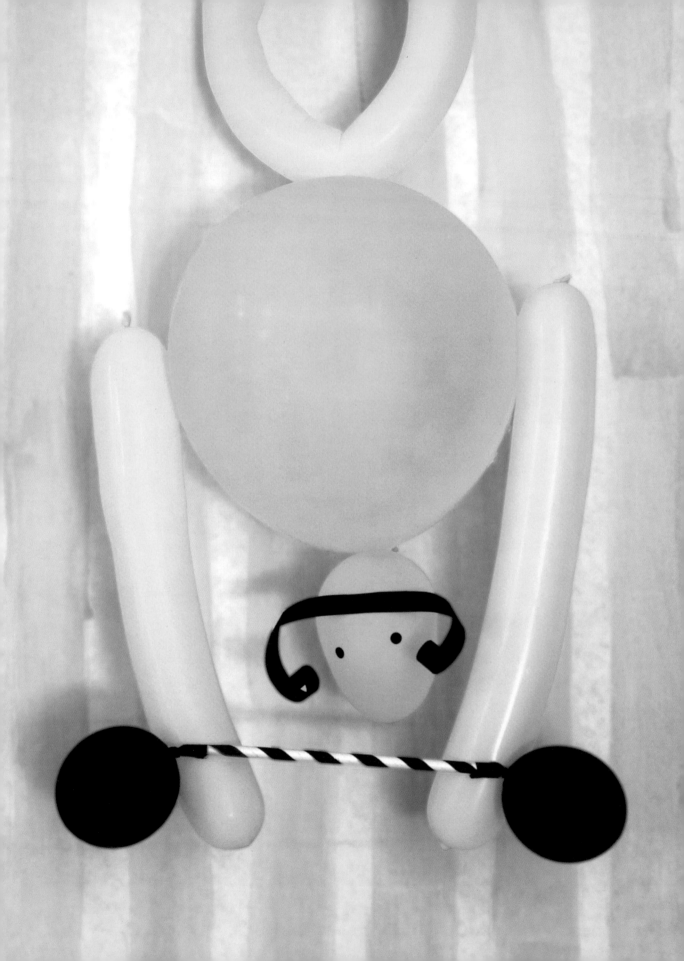

# LION CAKE TOPPER

A dyed coffee filter makes the perfect mane on this balloon lion! He is a fitting cake topper for a jungle- or zoo-themed party. If you want to make a freestanding lion, add feet by barely inflating four small yellow balloons (or four water balloons). Trim the knots and adhere each "foot" to the body with an adhesive dot.

**SUPPLIES**
**1 coffee filter, dyed yellow or orange**

**scissors**

**balloon pump**

**1 medium yellow balloon**

**1 yellow straw or skewer**

**adhesive dots (optional)**

**black permanent marker**

Dye a coffee filter yellow or orange (see page 14 for instructions). Cut out the center of the filter, leaving the ruffled outer circle intact.

**1.** Inflate the balloon so that the coffee filter will fit over it, as shown. Knot the balloon to a straw or skewer. Slip the ruffly ring onto the balloon so that the knot is at the back. If needed, slip some adhesive dots under the coffee filter ring to stick it to the balloon.

**2.** Have your child draw on a face with a permanent marker, or use stickers.

# GIRAFFE

This roly-poly giraffe would be a cute table decoration for a circus-, animal-, or safari-themed party.

**SUPPLIES**
**balloon pump**
**1 yellow twisty balloon**
**scissors**
**black dot stickers**
**2 yellow water balloons**
**adhesive dots**
**1 medium yellow balloon**
**2 yellow or yellow-striped straws, cut in half**

**1.** To make the head and neck, inflate the yellow twisty balloon while squeezing where you want it to bend to form the head. If that doesn't work, twist, bend, and release the head. Keep inflating the balloon to your desired thickness (even if it is too long). After it is fattened up, pinch off the length you want. Hold the pinch tightly and release the extra air. Knot the balloon where you are pinching it, and cut off the extra balloon.

**2.** To make the face, stick on two black dots for eyes and two black dots on the balloon tip for nostrils. For the ears and antlers, barely inflate the yellow water balloons so that they are tiny, and knot them. Attach them to the head with adhesive dots at the knot so that the balloons fold in half and the knotted ends stick up to become the antlers.

**3.** To make the torso, inflate the medium yellow balloon, and knot it. Trim the knot and cover it by attaching the bottom of the neck to the torso with one or two adhesive dots.

**4.** To make the legs, pinch the tops of the straw halves to flatten. Stick them to the torso with adhesive dots, splaying them out slightly for better stability.

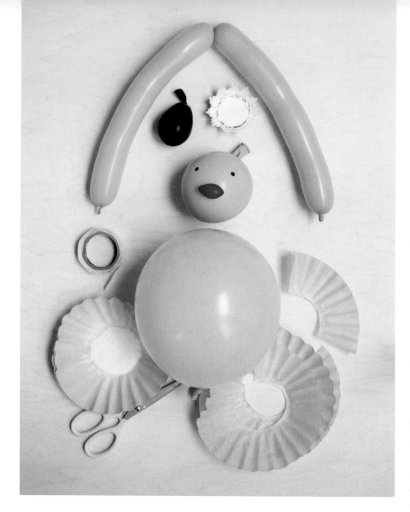

# BALLERINA

A whimsical balloon ballerina rests on top of a jar of cookies. She could also sit on a twisty balloon base, as with the clowns on page 58. Either way, she is the perfect table decoration for a sweet ballet-, pink-, or princess-themed party.

**SUPPLIES**
balloon pump

two medium pink balloons

scissors

8 coffee filters, dyed pink

adhesive dots

black dot stickers or permanent marker

1 silver cupcake paper

1 black water balloon (or whatever color you'd like the hair to be)

1 bright pink or red water balloon

1 pink twisty balloon (plus one more for a twisty balloon base; optional)

**1.** To make the body, inflate one of the 12" pink balloons and knot it.

**2.** To make the tutu, cut off the ruffly part of the pink coffee filters by cutting through a ruffled edge and cutting out the flat center. Cut the ruffles into 4- to 5-inch strips. Stick the ruffled strips to the center of the large balloon with the adhesive dots.

**3.** To make the head, slightly inflate the second pink balloon, and knot it. Trim the knot. Stick the dot stickers onto the face as eyes (see page 56 for eye techniques).

**4.** To make the crown, cut the center out of the silver cupcake paper. Trim the top into a zigzag shape, and stick the crown to the top of the head with an adhesive dot or two.

**5.** To make the hair, barely inflate the black balloon, knot it, and stick it to the head with adhesive dots just under the crown.

**6.** To make the lips, barely inflate the bright pink or red water balloon, knot it, and trim the knot. Stick the lips to the face with two adhesive dots, folding the knot under so that it is not visible.

**7.** To make the arms, inflate the pink twisty balloon, and knot it. Twist it at the center and hold. Stick each end of the balloon to the balloon body with an adhesive dot.

**8.** Rest her on the mouth of a large jar, or on a twisty balloon base formed into an O-shape, if desired. To make the base, inflate a matching-colored twisty balloon and curve into an O-shape. Hold in place before knotting to see if the round bottom of the ballerina's body will rest inside the O. Adjust the size, tie off, and adhere the ends together with an adhesive dot. Use adhesive dots to stick the bottom of the ballerina in the base.

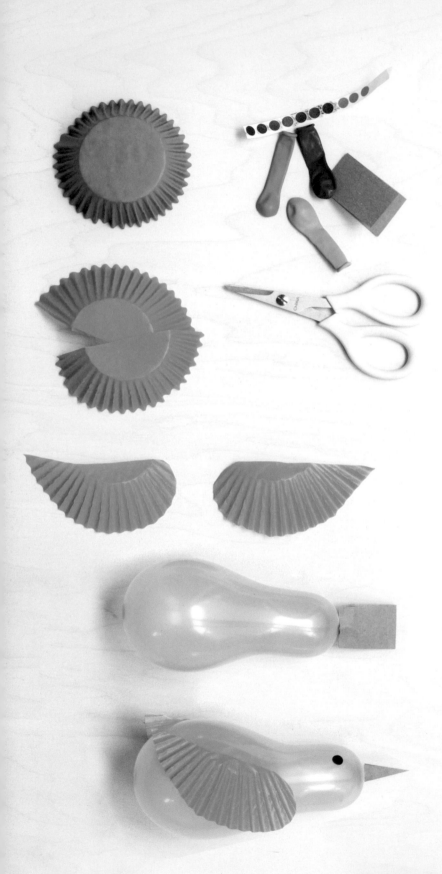

# BALLOON BIRDS

Craft a whole flock to fly over a party table, hanging these chubby little birds from balloon "clouds."

**SUPPLIES**

cupcake papers

scissors

balloon pump

water balloons

orange construction paper

double-sided tape

sticker dots (colored black) or a permanent marker

adhesive dots

thin string or twine

**1.** For the wings, cut a cupcake paper in half. Trim according to the template on page 100. (Flip the template to make left and right wings.)

**2.** Inflate a water balloon until it is about 4½" long. Knot and trim off the ends.

**3.** Cut the construction paper into two small rectangles about ¾" by 1" and sandwich the knot by using double-sided tape to affix the paper on either side of it. Carefully trim the paper into a triangular beak shape.

**4.** Add sticker eyes. Stick on the wings with adhesive dots, rounded sides toward the front.

**5.** To hang, add an adhesive dot to the top of the bird and press one end of the string onto the dot. Tie the other end of the string to the white balloon's knot.

# BALLOON FLOWERS

Once you get the hang of folding and cutting the paper petals for these flowers, making them goes really fast. They can be hung on a wall or grouped on a table. Start with any size squares of kraft paper or recycled paper bags.

**SUPPLIES**
**kraft paper or recycled paper bags, cut into squares ranging from 10" to 14"**

**scissors**

**balloon pump**

**regular round and water balloons**

**string (optional)**

**1.** Fold the paper squares in half and then in half again (into quarters). Fold diagonally in half again and then in half one last time.

**2.** Cut the open end into a half petal shape, as shown.

**3.** Open the flower. Poke a small hole in the center with the point of the scissors.

**4.** Inflate a balloon. Pull the knot through the hole in the center of the flower.

**5.** If you're hanging the flowers, tie a string to the knot behind the flower, and hang in a desired spot.

# BALLOON PLANETS

These balloon planets are easy to make. Kids will have fun helping to paint them.

**SUPPLIES**
pencil

scrap corrugated cardboard from a large box, or the clean top of a pizza box

scissors

acrylic paint

paintbrushes

balloon pump

any size round balloons

string

clothespins

**1.** To make Saturn's ring, trace a large circle on the cardboard and a smaller circle inside the larger one. Cut out the ring. Paint it, making stripes as shown. Let it dry.

**2.** Inflate a variety of colors of balloons to different sizes. (If you don't have different-sized balloons, just inflate some more than others.)

**3.** To make Saturn, rest the cardboard ring over the edge of a table and a chair (or have a friend hold it), and inflate the balloon right into the center.

Overinflate the balloon slightly so that it stays snug in the ring.

**4.** Hang up a string. Clip the balloons by their knot to the string with the clothespins. Paint each balloon planet and let dry.

**5.** Once dry, the planets can be displayed by hanging them from individual strings or along one long string. Knot or clip the balloons to the string.

# TWISTY BALLOON LETTERS

Create a big, bright, happy message with twisty balloon letters! There are a few ways to make these. Using clear adhesive dots is essential to each technique.

**SUPPLIES**

**pencil and paper**

**balloon pump**

**twisty balloons**

**scissors**

**clear adhesive dots**

**1.** Sketch out your message and what colors each balloon segment will be so you know how many balloons you will need for each letter. Some simpler letters (like *I, P,* and *D*) can be made with only one balloon.

**2.** Inflate the balloon to get the thickness that you want. Pinch the balloon where you want the length to end, and release air from that point only. Knot the balloon at the pinched spot, and cut off the excess balloon.

**3.** For letters with straight lines and no curves or twists (like *H* and *T*), each line is adhered with an adhesive dot where the line segments touch.

**4.** For simple curved letters, like *P* and *D,* twist at the point that the line needs to turn, curve the balloon around, and adhere the end with an adhesive dot.

**5.** *B* and *R:* Start by making a *P* (see step 4). To make a *B:* Inflate a short length of balloon and knot. Curve it into a backward C-shape, and adhere both ends to the *P* with sticky dots. Similarly, to make an *R:* Add a short diagonal line to a *P* with an adhesive dot.

**6.** *A* and *Y:* Make a V-shape by twisting the middle of the balloon and adding an adhesive dot on the inside of the twist. For the *A*, add a short straight balloon inside the *V* with adhesive dots. For the *Y*, add a short straight balloon to the bottom of the *V* with adhesive dots.

**LIKE MANY ARTISTS** and crafters, I've always had a special place in my heart for cardboard. **As a kid, I saved every piece of cardboard** that came out of my dad's new shirts, every glove insert, shoebox, matchbox, egg carton—you name it. In one of my favorite craft books was a dreamy playhouse made from a corrugated-cardboard refrigerator box with a side tunnel constructed out of many boxes glued together. I waited and waited for that refrigerator box to materialize on a street corner but never found one. So I scaled down and made tiny shoebox houses with matchbox beds for my dolls.

Even now, with so many craft supplies and kits available, **people still love found materials,** the look of cardboard, and the idea of transforming common materials like toilet paper tubes.

**Cardboard tubes—there is never a reason to throw out these gems.** Always keep a stash for yourself for sculptures, lightsabers, telescopes, and the projects on these pages. Many elementary school art teachers will be happy to have you deliver a bag of collected tubes to them. Save all different kinds (toilet paper, paper towel, gift wrap, plastic wrap, aluminum foil) for a variety of sizes and weights.

In addition to these usual suspects, hold onto packaging from colorful coated boxes (such as cereal boxes) for projects that use their graphics, like the pop-up cards on page 76.

# RECYCLED BOX POP-UP CARDS

### HEART GARLAND CARD

*The garland on this card can hold pennants, flags, letters, or any hand-cut or craft-punched shapes.*

**SUPPLIES**

**scissors**

**1 cardboard or cardstock card (plus 1 more for backing; optional)**

**twine or thin string**

**waxed or scrap paper**

**white glue**

**scraps of cardboard packaging cut into heart shapes**

**markers (optional)**

**sticker letters (optional)**

**1.** Cut a slit in the top two corners of one of the cards.

**2.** Cut a piece of string to your desired garland length, plus 2" extra. Lay your string down on top of the waxed paper, and glue the cut heart shapes onto the string, leaving 1" on each side of the string uncovered. Let dry.

**3.** Thread each end of the string into each slit. Glue or knot the ends of the string behind the card.

**4.** Glue the second card onto the back to cover the strings, if desired, using a very thin layer of white glue.

**5.** Add a handwritten or sticker-letter greeting.

# CITYSCAPE CARD

*This cityscape is made on a basic pop-up card base. By gluing on different shapes, this foundation can be used for many different types of pop-up cards.*

## SUPPLIES

**1 folded cardboard or cardstock card, around 6" × 8" (plus 1 more for backing; optional)**

**scissors**

**craft knife and ruler (optional)**

**white glue**

**scraps of cardboard packaging cut into building shapes or into triangles for "trees"**

**1.** To make a basic pop-up base, start with the card folded. Use scissors or a craft knife and a ruler to make parallel pairs of slits (this card calls for five) perpendicular to the fold. Vary the lengths of the slits so that when popped out, they will be staggered, but keep them shorter than half the depth of the card so they won't poke out when the card is folded. Pop the slits forward inside the card to make tabs for gluing (as shown opposite).

**2.** Glue the building shapes to only one side of the tabs. (With the card sitting open, attach to the side of the tabs facing you, not the top of the tabs.) Keep the shapes shorter than half the card's depth if you don't want them to poke out.

**3.** Glue the outside of the pop-out card to the inside of the second card to hide the slits, if desired, using a very thin layer of white glue.

# GIANT BOX BLOCKS

Playing with blocks is the best! These cardboard blocks, made from recycled boxes, are great as an instant fort, bridge, or town.

**SUPPLIES**
**assorted large boxes**
**hot glue**
**newspaper or drop cloth**
**paint**
**paintbrushes**

**1.** If your boxes have too much printing on them and you'd like a plain box, you can turn them inside out. If your boxes are already flattened (box flaps flipped open at each end), you are halfway there. If not, remove the tape and open the flaps. Find the glued seam at one edge of the box, and peel it open. Your box should be completely flatten-able now. Reglue the other side of the flap that you just opened so that the box will be inside out. Glue the flaps closed.

**2.** Spread the newspaper out on the floor, and put the boxes on it. Paint the sides of the boxes solid colors, or paint letters, geometric shapes, or anything you'd like. Let them dry completely.

# BIG BOX TOWN

These components are modular, and can be moved around by young city planners who like to rethink and redesign their town layout.

**SUPPLIES**
**assorted large boxes**

**utility knife or scissors**

**hot glue**

**pencil**

**newspaper or drop cloth**

**paint**

**paintbrushes**

**small sponge**

**toilet paper tubes**

**1.** If your boxes have too much printing on them and you'd like a plain box, you can turn them inside out. (See step 1 in Giant Box Blocks, page 78.)

**2.** To make a pitched (pointy) roof, the wide flaps will be the two sides of the roof. (Let the smaller side flaps flop open for now.) Use a utility knife to carefully cut down the same length into all four box edges to lengthen the flaps to your desired roof length. Make a new fold to bend the roof flaps down to meet. Hot-glue the top edges together. Lift up a side flap and place it against the side of the roof. Trace the roof angle onto the side flap, and cut it with a utility knife or scissors to make it pointy. Test to see if it will fit under the roof once it's flipped up. Trim as needed. Run a thin line of hot glue along the top edge of the side flap and press it under the roof. Repeat for the other side.

**3.** To make a steeple, as on the red-and-orange building pictured, make a skinny pitched-top box, and cut it open at the bottom. Put the bottom side against the pitched roof it will sit on top of, and trace that roof angle. Cut an upside-down V-shape out of the bottom so it can rest on the pitched roof. Repeat on the other side. Trim as needed.

**4.** Spread the newspaper out on the floor, and put the boxes on it. Paint the boxes and let them dry.

**5.** Use the sponge's side and gray paint to stamp skinny rectangles onto the buildings, or cut it to stamp square or rectangular windows.

**6.** To make a scalloped, tiled roof, as on the dark blue house, cut a toilet paper tube in half the long way, dip the edge into paint, and stamp on semicircles.

**7.** Glue on cardboard details like doors. Make toilet-paper-tube chimneys by cutting the bottom at an angle to fit on a pitched roof, as shown.

**8.** Use your own toys, such as cars, racetracks, and animals, as props in the town.

# BOX VILLAGE

My boys and I made this recycled box village a few years ago.
We had fun, and I loved having this on our mantel for the whole holiday
season. There is some prep work required before you get
the kids involved, but it's worth it. It is magical, glowing at night.

A

B

## SUPPLIES

**assorted empty boxes and containers, such as milk cartons and cereal, cracker, and tissue boxes**

**craft knife**

**masking or white artist's tape**

**hot or white glue**

**pencil**

**scissors (optional)**

**gesso (white acrylic primer) or white acrylic paint**

**paintbrushes**

**acrylic craft paint or poster paint**

**waxed paper**

**battery-operated tea lights**

**green cupcake papers (optional)**

**branches (optional)**

**gumdrops or clay**

**nut cups, small and large (optional)**

**1.** Prepare the boxes and containers by using a craft knife to cut out any plastic spouts from the milk cartons, then taping over the holes. Glue shut all open box flaps (A) unless you plan on making pitched roofs.

**2.** To make a pitched roof, choose which sides will be the two angled sides of the roof. (Let the other sides flop open for now.) Use a craft knife to lengthen the flaps to your desired roof length by carefully cutting down the corners. Make a new fold to bend the roof flaps down so they meet and hot glue the top edges together. Lift up an unglued side flap and place it against the side of the glued roof. Trace the roof angle onto the side flap and cut it with scissors or a utility knife to make it pointy. Test to see if it will fit under the roof. Trim as needed. Run a thin line of hot glue along the top edge of the side flap and press it under the roof. Repeat for the other side.

**3.** Prime the boxes with the gesso (B). (If you use white acrylic paint instead, you might need two coats.) Let dry.

**4.** Paint the buildings, making sure to add lots of windows and snowy roofs. Let dry.

**5.** Using the craft knife (adults only), carefully cut out the insides of the windows. (I repeat, be careful!)

**6.** Use scissors or the craft knife to cut out the bottoms of the buildings. Cut rectangular holes or flaps for the doors.

**7.** Cut a piece of waxed paper large enough to cover all the cut window openings. Brush white glue around the windows inside the box and press the waxed paper onto the glue.

**8.** Line up the boxes in a nice townlike arrangement. Place one or two battery-operated tea lights in each house.

**9.** For a pretty mantel display, make some leafy branches: Collect a few dried tree branches and, using the leaf template on page 100, cut leaf shapes out of the cupcake papers. Hot-glue a few leaves to each branch. Anchor each branch by poking the bottom into a gumdrop or a nut cup filled with clay or gumdrops.

# TUBE ANIMALS

The charm of these animals is that they are still paper towel tubes—cylindrical and raw cardboard brown. Older kids handy with scissors can make these creatures (see the templates on pages 102–103). (Adults should handle any cuts made with the utility knife.) Once they see how many ways there are to cut cardboard tubes, they will come up with tons of ideas of their own! Create a habitat by cutting paper watering holes and cardboard trees.

*The eyes are made by hole-punching black construction paper. To glue on tiny circles and other shapes, dot glue onto the tube with a toothpick. Alternatively, the features can be drawn on with a marker.*

**SUPPLIES**
**scissors**

**paper towel tubes**

**pencil**

**small pieces of scrap cardboard**

**craft knife**

**black paper or a black marker**

**⅛" hole punch**

**white glue and adhesive dots (optional)**

## LION

**1.** Enlarge the lion template (see the templates on page 103) as instructed. Cut out and wrap the shape around a paper towel tube. Lightly trace the template. Cut out the lion shape. Fold the fringes back for the mane.

**2.** To make the face, trace a circle onto scrap cardboard, using the uncut side of the tube as a template. Cut the circle out inside the traced line. Glue or draw on eyes, a small triangular nose, and a mouth. Squeeze a thin line of glue just inside the tube at the mane end and fit the circle into the tube, as shown.

**3.** To make the legs, cut off two ⅜" strips of another paper towel tube. Taper the cut ends of both the strips. Glue each set of legs under the lion's torso.

**4.** Fold up the tail.

## MONKEY

**1.** Enlarge the monkey template (see the templates on page 103) as instructed. Cut out and wrap the shape around a paper towel tube. Lightly trace the template.

**2.** Cut out the monkey shape. Use a craft knife to carefully saw into the tube, as needed, for areas that are hard to reach with scissors (like between the monkey's legs). Cut the snout out of a scrap from the tube.

**3.** Bend the neck down and then bend the head up at the chin. Glue or draw on eyes. Affix the snout with an adhesive dot.

**4.** Bend the arms, hands, legs, and tail as indicated on the template.

## ANTELOPE

**1.** Enlarge the antelope and antlers templates (see the templates on page 103) as instructed. Cut out and wrap the template around a paper towel tube. Lightly trace the template. Trace the antler shapes onto scrap cardboard or another tube.

**2.** Cut out the antelope and antler shapes. Use a craft knife to carefully saw into the tube for areas that are hard to reach with scissors (like between the antelope's legs).

**3.** Fold the legs and tail as indicated on the template.

**4.** Glue on antlers, and fold at the center. Glue or draw on eyes.

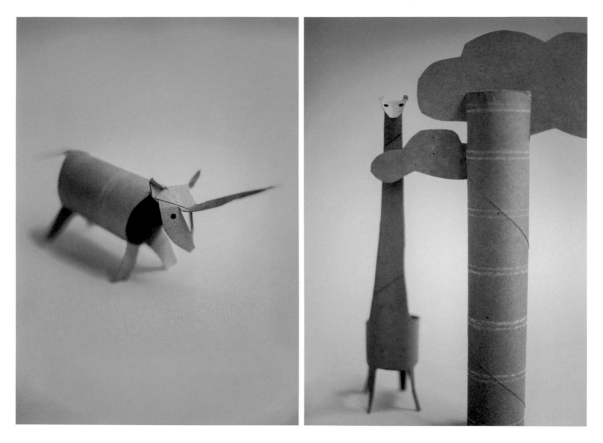

## RHINOCEROS

**1.** Enlarge the rhinoceros template (see the template on page 102) as instructed. Cut out and wrap the shape around a paper towel tube. Lightly trace the template.

**2.** Cut out the rhinoceros shape.

**3.** Fold the legs and tail as indicated on the template. Fold up the horn, and pinch the ears to fold the edges up, as shown.

**4.** Glue or draw on eyes. Overlap the split bottom of the chin and glue in place.

## GIRAFFE

**1.** Enlarge the giraffe template (see the template on page 102) as instructed. Cut out and wrap the shape around a paper towel tube. Lightly trace the template.

**2.** Use a craft knife to make a starter hole in the tube where it is hard for scissors to reach. Cut out the giraffe shape. Fold down the head, fold up the ears, and glue or draw on eyes.

## ELEPHANT

**1.** Enlarge the elephant template (see the template on page 102) as instructed. Cut out and wrap the shape around a paper towel tube. Lightly trace the template.

**2.** Cut out the elephant shape. Use a craft knife to carefully saw into the tube for the ears. Fold the ears forward. Glue or draw on eyes.

**3.** To make the legs, cut a ½" ring off another paper towel tube. Cut the ring in half. Glue the legs under the elephant's torso, as shown.

**4.** For a baby elephant, shorten the torso length and cut the legs shorter.

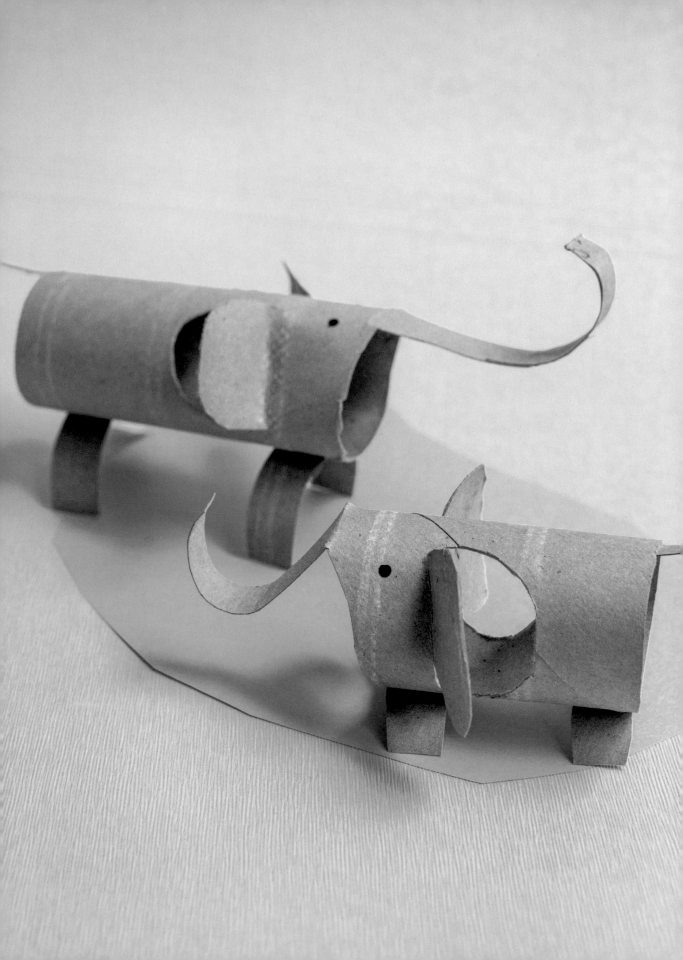

# SEA CREATURES MOBILE

This mobile would be sweet hung in a nursery or above a table at an under-the-sea party. Using pinking shears adds spikiness to the fish fins and is a quick way to give the shark a mouthful of teeth!

**SUPPLIES**

**paper towel tubes**

**scissors**

**pencil**

**scrap cardboard (like an empty cereal box)**

**pinking shears (optional)**

**craft knife**

**white glue**

**paint**

**paintbrush**

**⅛" hole punch**

**black paper (or a black marker)**

**large sewing needle, such as a tapestry or darning needle**

**baker's twine**

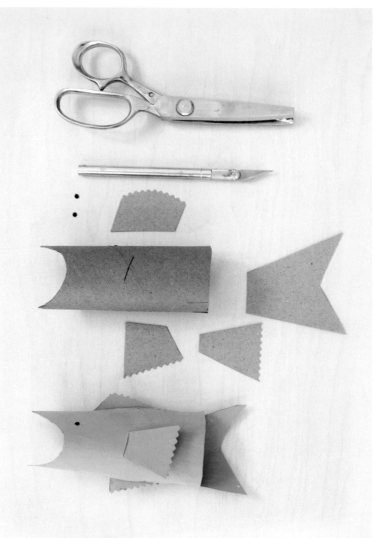

## FISH

**1.** Enlarge the fish, fin, and tail templates (see the templates on page 104) as instructed. Cut out the fish template, and wrap the shape around a paper towel tube. Lightly trace the template. Cut out the fish shape.

**2.** On the scrap cardboard, trace and cut out two side fins, top and bottom fins, and a tail fin, using pinking shears for a zigzag edge, if desired.

**3.** Use a craft knife to cut slits as indicated on the template. Slide the fins into their slits. Squeeze a thin line of glue where the fins meet the slits, and wipe off excess glue. Let dry.

**4.** When the glue is dry, paint inside (as far as you can reach) dark pink and the outside blue.

**5.** Hole-punch black paper to make eyes. Once the paint is dry, glue or draw on eyes.

## SHARK

**1.** Enlarge the shark, fin, and tail templates (see the templates on page 105) as instructed. Cut out the shark template and wrap the shape around a paper towel tube. Lightly trace the template. Cut out the shape, using pinking shears for the teeth, if desired.

**2.** On the scrap cardboard, trace and cut out the top fin and a tail fin.

**3.** Use scissors to cut slits as indicated on the template for the tail, and use the craft knife to cut slits for the top fin and side gills. Slide the fins into their slits. Squeeze a thin line of glue where the fins meet the slits, and wipe off excess glue. Fold up the top gill. Let dry.

**4.** When the glue is dry, paint the inside (as far as you can reach) pink, the outside gray, and the teeth white.

**5.** Hole-punch black paper to make eyes. Once the paint is dry, glue or draw on eyes.

## OCTOPUS

**1.** Enlarge the octopus template (see the templates on page 104) as indicated. Cut out and wrap the shape around a paper towel tube. Lightly trace the template.

**2.** Cut out the octopus shape. Squeeze the top of the head together and cut the two sides of the rounded head at once.

**3.** Open the top of the head, squeeze a line of glue on the inside edge of the top of the head, and squeeze closed again. Hold in place for a few minutes or use a clothespin

or binder clip to hold it closed. Let dry.

**4.** Curl the legs up, as shown, by wrapping around a pencil.

**5.** Paint the octopus.

**6.** Hole-punch black paper to make eyes. Once the paint is dry, glue or draw on eyes.

## MOBILE STRINGING INSTRUCTIONS

**1.** Use a sewing needle to poke a hole in the center bottom of the shark, as indicted on the template. Poke another hole down through the top center of the glued seam of the octopus head.

**2.** Thread the needle with a 20" piece of string. Knot it at the end, and thread it up through

the bottom of the octopus, through the hole in the head seam. Gently pull the string up until the knot hits the inside edge.

**3.** Poke the needle into the hole on the bottom of the shark, and bring the needle up through the top fin slit. Slide the shark down the string to space it about 2" from the octopus, and bring the needle up through the bottom of the fish, in the bottom fin slit and up through the top fin slit. Slide the fish down the string so it is about 1½" to 2" above the shark.

**4.** If the creatures are slipping on the string, put on a bit of glue at the top of each string hole. Let dry and hang.

# TUBE LETTERS

Cardboard tube letters are a graphic way to display a message on a mantel, shelf, or party table. Once you get the hang of cutting out these letters, you can create your own to spell out a name or even a whole alphabet as an educational craft. Instead of toilet paper tubes, you can also use paper towel tubes, cut to the desired length.

**SUPPLIES**
**scissors**
**toilet paper tubes**
**double-sided tape**
**craft knife**
**craft paint in various colors**
**paintbrush**
**primer (optional)**

**1.** Trim the letter templates on page 108, leaving about a ¼" border along the sides with the dotted line. Tape the template to the tube.

**2.** Trim the letter along the dotted "cut" lines. Lift one side of the template off, leaving the other side taped on. Fold the letter at the dotted line on the taped-on side. Flip over the untaped side to create a mirror-image template on the back of the tube and tape it in place. Use the scissors to neaten your cuts, if necessary.

**3.** Paint the tubes and let them dry. (Optional: Paint with a primer first to give your letters a more vibrant color.)

**4.** Tip for creating other letters: For one-sided, asymmetrical cuts at the base of the tube (as on the letter *P* or *B*), more than half the tube must remain uncut at the base or the letter will tip over.

# GOLD LEAF NAPKIN RINGS

These napkin rings would look pretty on a Thanksgiving table or at a golden anniversary party.

**1.** Paint cardboard scraps gold and let dry.

**2.** Cut the cardboard into rectangles 1½" long, and fold them in half along the ridges. Cut out leaf shapes.

**3.** Cut the paper towel tube into rings ½" wide. (You may find it easier to saw rings off using a craft knife, but be careful doing this.)

**4.** Hot-glue the leaves onto the rings, as shown.

# GOLD LEAF DESSERT STAND

A little gold paint dresses up this dessert stand made from toilet paper tubes and a bunch of cardboard scraps!

**1.** The 5½" diameter circle will be the base.

**2.** Cut the toilet paper tubes, if needed, so that one of them is 3½" tall and two are 4" tall.

**3.** Use a ruler to find the center on the bottom of each cardboard circle, and lightly mark the spot with a pencil.

**4.** Glue the shortest tube to the base, making sure to center the tube on the circle. Glue the other end of the tube to the 11" circle. Glue a 4" tube onto the other side of the 11" circle, and then glue the other end of the tube to the 9" circle. Glue the second 4" tube onto the other side of the 9" circle, and then glue the other end of the tube onto the 5" circle.

**5.** Paint the dessert stand gold after gluing so you hide the glue. Let dry.

**6.** Hot-glue the leaves to the cardboard strips. Hot-glue the leaf-covered strips around the edges of each layer.

# TUBE MENORAH

A sturdy tube like the kind found inside a roll of aluminum foil or wrapping paper is ideal for this project, though a paper towel tube works fine too!

**SUPPLIES**
pencil

1 skinny cardboard tube (see above), about 12" long

ruler

craft knife

1 paper towel tube, cut down to 4"

scissors

5 straws

white glue

one 3" corrugated cardboard circle

silver paint

paintbrush

9 yellow spice drops

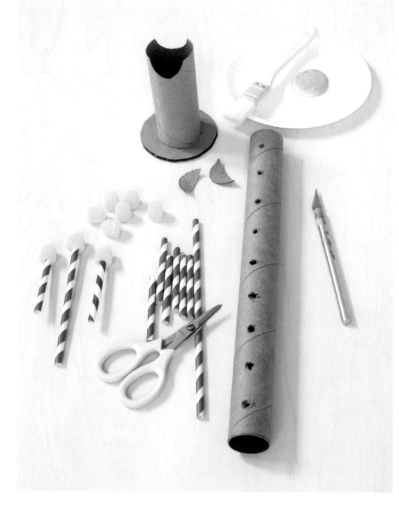

**1.** Mark the center dot on the long cardboard tube. Measure and mark four evenly spaced dots on either side of the center (they should be around 1¼" apart).

**2.** Carefully poke the tip of the craft knife into the tube at one of the dots, and cut out a small starter hole, spinning the knife around to enlarge the hole. Put a straw into the hole to see if the size is right. The fit should be a bit snug. Repeat with the remaining dots.

**3.** Hold one end of the long tube to the top side of the 4" tube, and trace a semicircle to make a spot where the long tube can rest. Cut out the semicircle, and use the scrap as a template to mark and cut a semicircle directly on the other side.

**4.** Glue the uncut side of the short tube to the center of the cardboard disc to make the base. Let dry.

**5.** Glue the long tube onto the base, centered. Let dry.

**6.** Paint the menorah silver.

**7.** Cut 4 straws in half and one down to 6" to make "candles."

To make "flames," poke the straws into the flat bottom of yellow spice drops.

**8.** Have your child add a straw candle each night of Hanukkah.

# SANTA TUBE FAVOR BOX

There is a lot of snipping for these little favor boxes, but making them will go quickly if you cut multiples of all the pieces, assembly-line style, using the templates (see page 101). They are two-part boxes: one tube will serve as the inside sleeve and the other tube will become the outside Santa covering. Fill them with little toys and wrapped candies.

side down, on the scrap cardboard and trace two circles. Cut one circle inside the traced line; this is for the top of Santa's head. Test to see if it is a snug fit in the Santa tube. Glue the circle inside the cut top of the tube to seal it. Cut the other circle outside the traced line to make a larger circle; set this aside for the base.

**2.** To make the inside tube base, cut ½" off the length of the second toilet paper tube to shorten it. Cut the tube open lengthwise, overlap the ends about ¼", and glue it closed. (Alternatively, if you have any skinnier tubes, such as from gift wrap, plastic wrap, or aluminum foil, or even from a different brand of toilet paper, those work well just as they are.) Glue this tube to the base circle, as shown.

**3.** Cut all the Santa clothes out of paper, using the templates, and glue them on as shown (red pieces first, then white center stripe, then black belt). Cut the beard and hat fur out of ruffled cupcake paper, using the templates, and glue them on. Add the eyes.

**4.** Fill the base with treats, and slide Santa over the base.

**SUPPLIES**
scissors

**2 toilet paper tubes**

**small scrap piece of cardboard**

**pencil**

**white and/or hot glue**

**red-, white-, and black-colored paper**

**1 white cupcake paper**

**small hole punch (¹⁄₁₆" or ¹⁄₈")
or a marker (for eyes)**

**1.** Enlarge and cut out all the Santa templates (see page 101). Wrap the Santa body template around one of the tubes and cut the pointy hat shape. Place that tube, uncut

# TEMPLATES

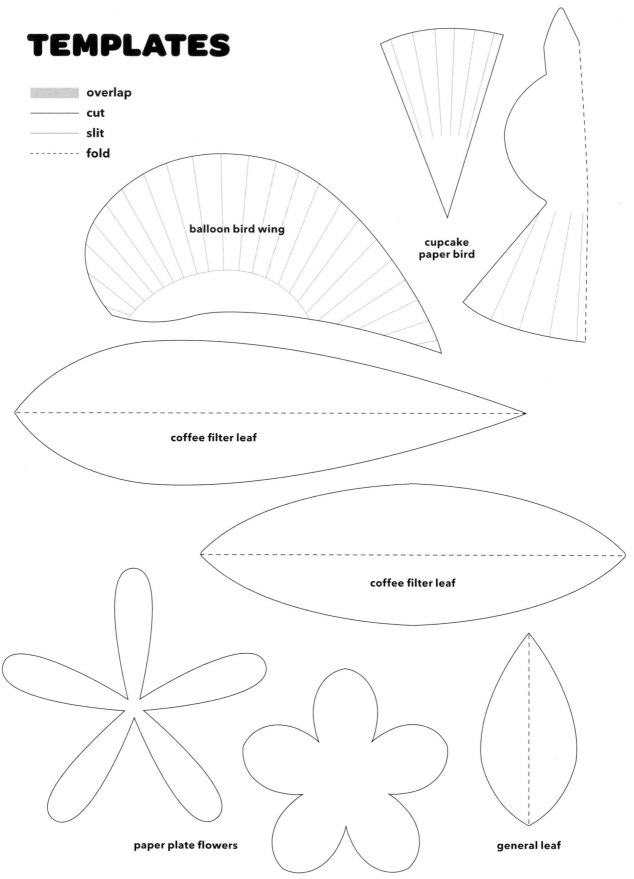

overlap

cut

slit

fold

balloon bird wing

cupcake
paper bird

coffee filter leaf

coffee filter leaf

paper plate flowers

general leaf

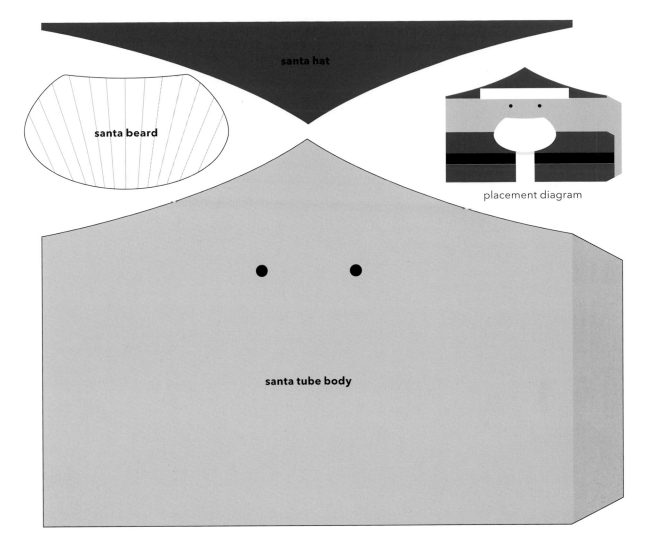

santa hat

santa beard

placement diagram

santa tube body

santa belt

santa jacket

santa hat fur

santa jacket fur

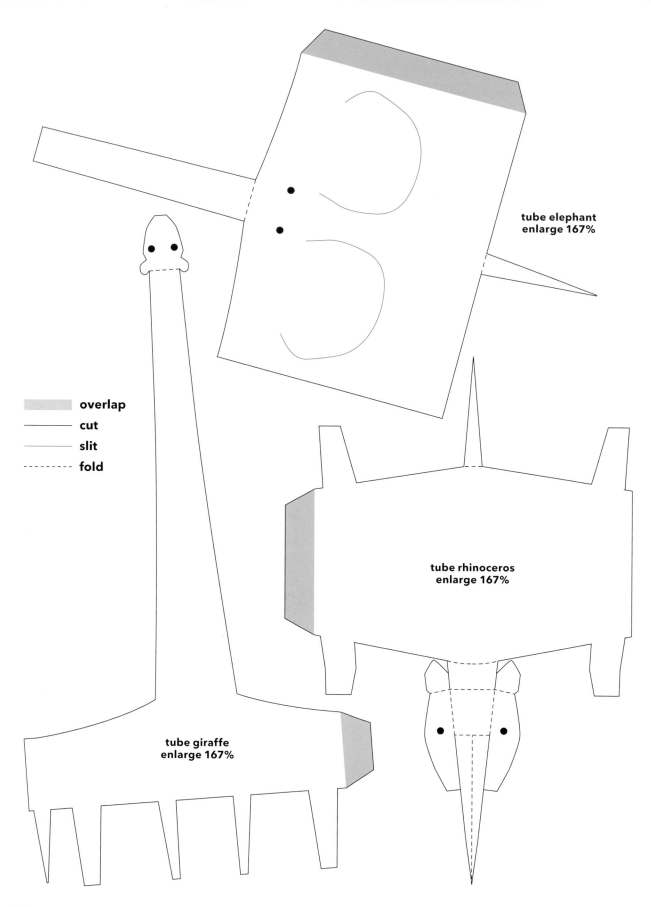

overlap

cut

slit

fold

tube elephant
enlarge 167%

tube rhinoceros
enlarge 167%

tube giraffe
enlarge 167%

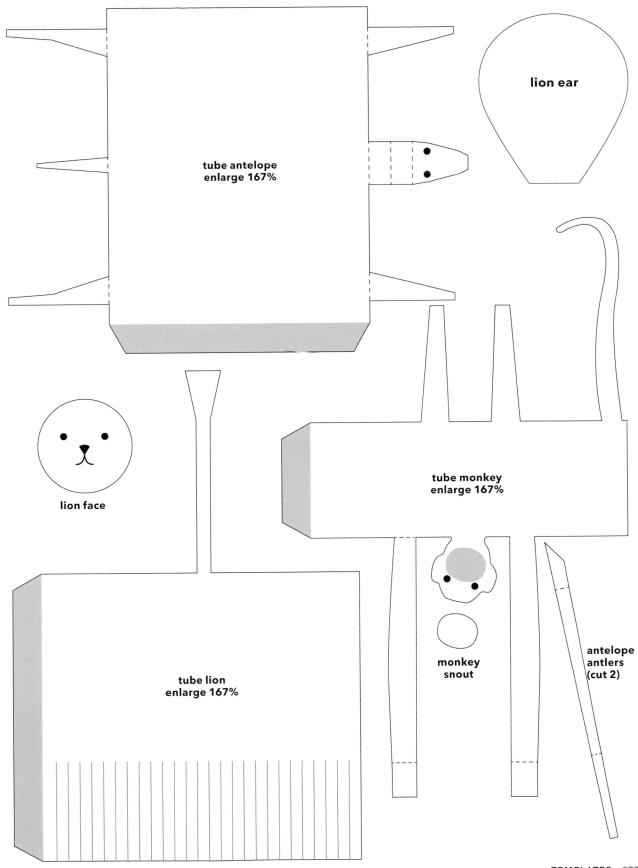

lion ear

tube antelope
enlarge 167%

lion face

tube monkey
enlarge 167%

tube lion
enlarge 167%

monkey
snout

antelope
antlers
(cut 2)

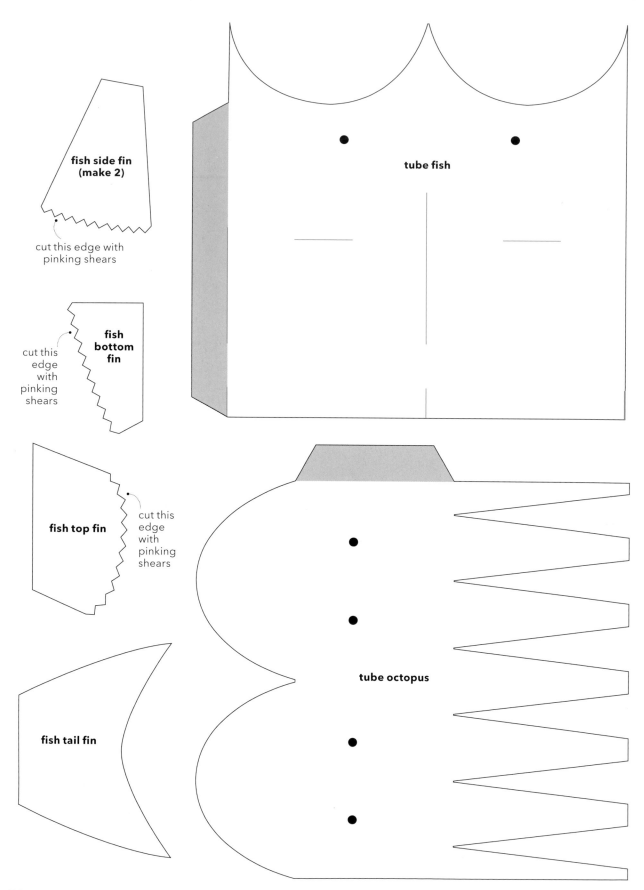

**fish side fin (make 2)**

cut this edge with pinking shears

**fish bottom fin**

cut this edge with pinking shears

**fish top fin**

cut this edge with pinking shears

**fish tail fin**

**tube fish**

**tube octopus**

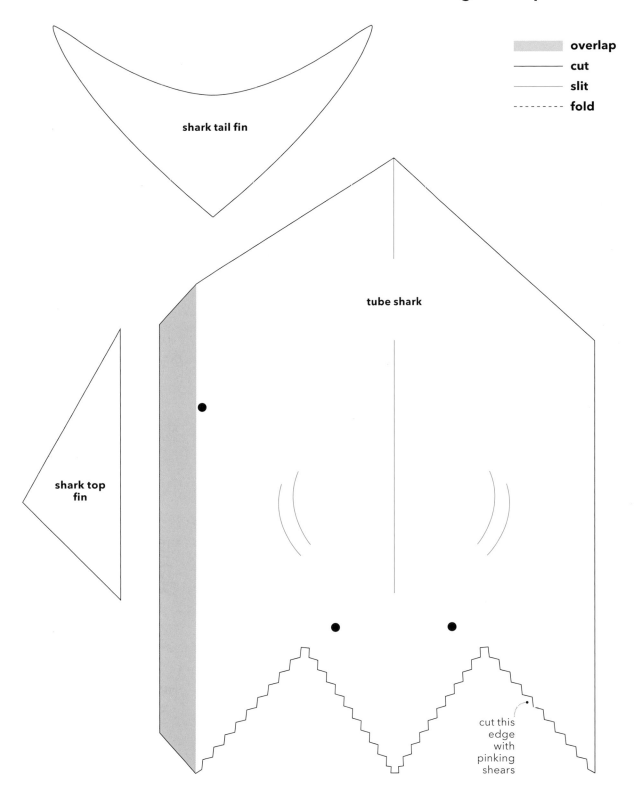

**Enlarge all templates 133%**

overlap
cut
slit
-------- fold

shark tail fin

tube shark

shark top fin

cut this edge with pinking shears

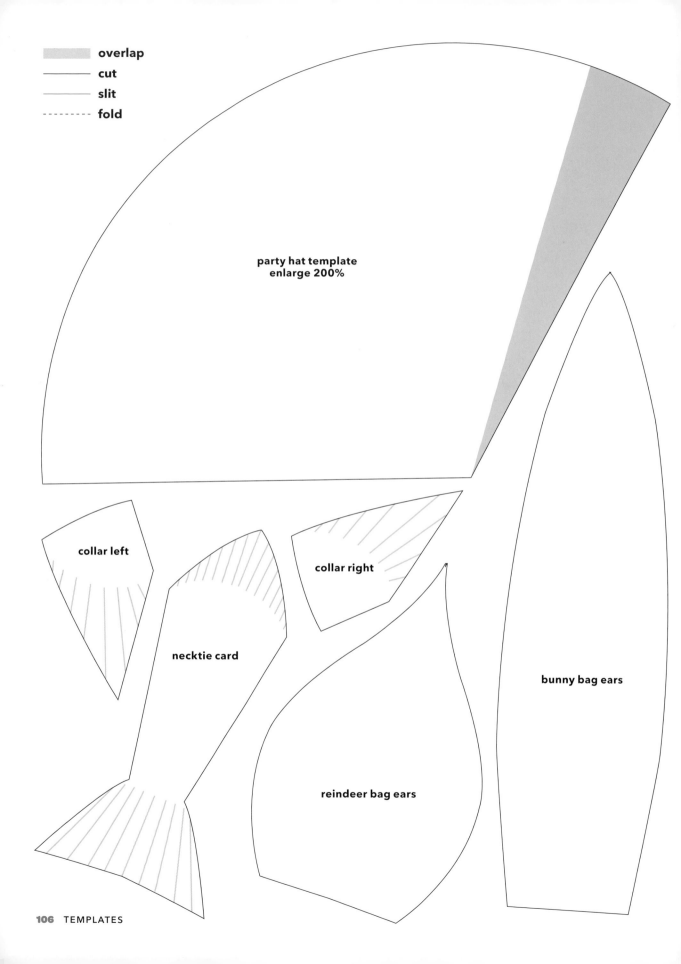

overlap

cut

slit

fold

party hat template
enlarge 200%

collar left

collar right

necktie card

bunny bag ears

reindeer bag ears

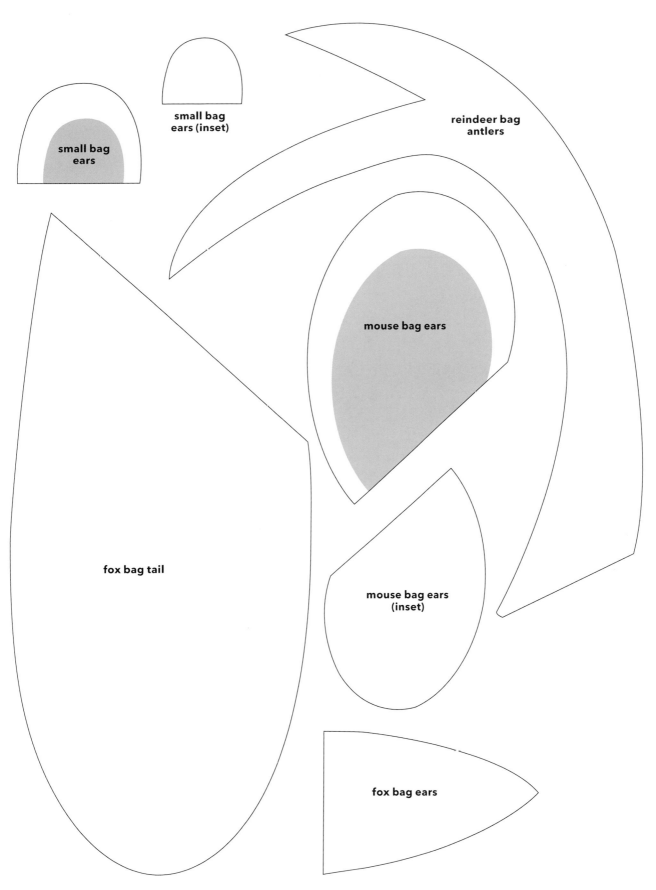

small bag ears

small bag
ears (inset)

reindeer bag
antlers

mouse bag ears

fox bag tail

mouse bag ears
(inset)

fox bag ears

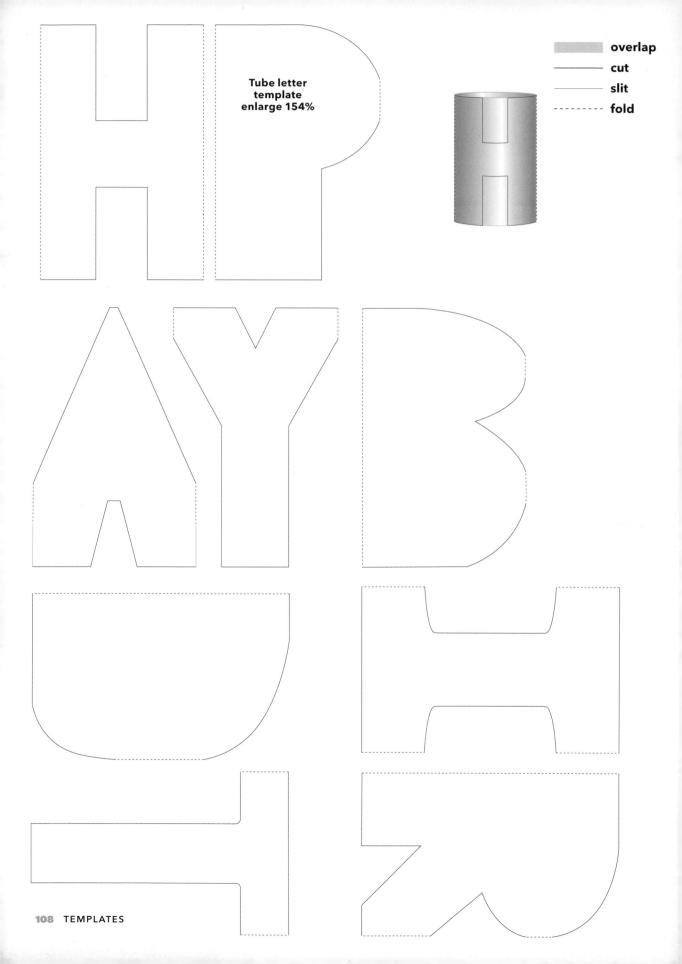

Tube letter
template
enlarge 154%

overlap
cut
slit
fold

# ACKNOWLEDGMENTS

**THANK YOU** to the wonderful team at Potter Craft: our editor, Ashley Phillips, Stephanie Huntwork, Sigi Nacson, Phil Leung, Aaron Wehner, Doris Cooper, Pam Krauss, Erica Gelbard, and Kevin Sweeting.

To our amazing agent, Carla Glasser.

And special thanks to our friend and brilliant designer Robin Rosenthal, photo technician David Miao, and our dear friend Margaret McCartney, who helped us in so many ways, including crafting and template-making.

Jordan Ferney, we are honored by and grateful for your thoughtful and sweet foreword.

To Jodi's family: Fred, my inspirer, coach, and love of my life, thank you for so many things! My sweet boys, Sammy and Lionel; my incredible parents, Adele and Sheldon Levine; my mother-in-law, RoseMary Muench;

David Levine and Mary Oleszek, Katharine and Greg Nemec, Allison and JP Williams. Jacob, Olivia, Piper, Margaret, Alexander, Eve, and Connie! And Simone Gomes.

And to Amy's family: Adam, Oliver, Owen, and Beatrice; Lauren, Ben, Lila and Noah Lowry; and Lou and Jane Gropp.

Dearest friends, including (but not limited to!): Annette Berry, Johanna Goodman, Jordin Isip, Melissa McGill, Melinda Beck, Noel Claro, Page Marchese Norman, Paul Slifer, Sophie Glasser, Helen Quinn, Debra Goldman, Tracey Stewart, Lisel Ashlock, Rachel Filler, and Gerald Pindus.

Thank you for your support Yolanda Edwards, Rachel Faucett, Jenny Rosenstrach, Martha Stewart, Gael Towey, Ellen Morrissey, Eric Pike, Darcy Miller, Hannah Milman, Marcie McGoldrick, Silke Stoddard, and so many *Martha Stewart Living* friends.

# INDEX